RECEPTION TO GOD'S ASSEMBLY

GW00569773

Reception to God's Assembly

WILLIAM BUNTING

JOHN RITCHIE LTD
CHRISTIAN PUBLICATIONS

40 Beansburn, Kilmarnock, Scotland

ISBN 0 946351 33 3

Typeset by John Ritchie Ltd., Kilmarnock
Printed by Bell & Bain Ltd., Glasgow

"Prove all things;
Hold fast that which is good." - 1 Thess. 5:21.
"If any man willeth to do His will, he shall know
of the teaching, whether it be of God, or whether
I speak from Myself." - John 7:17 (R.V.)

Reception to God's Assembly

Foreword

Assembly fellowship is characterised by the enjoyment and exercise of many divinely bestowed privileges and responsibilities.

Entry into such a spiritual sphere is the culmination of preceding steps of obedience and conviction. Those who were added to the assembly in Acts 2:41, had first 'received His word' and 'been baptised'. It should also be noted that having been added, they continued steadfastly in the spiritual activities and exercises of the assembly. The modern concepts of 'occasional fellowship' and 'Sunday morning only' attendance find no basis in the Word of God.

The New Testament gives examples of those who are in the family of God, but not in the fellowship of a local assembly. The moral offender in 1 Cor. 5 was to be 'put away' from the assembly, thus he was still a 'born again' believer, but not in local assembly fellowship until he would repent and be received back in again.

The late Mr William Bunting was a well known and respected teacher of the Word of God, as well as being an evangelist. He was a thoughtful student of the Scripture and having led many to Christ through preaching, was careful to teach them the 'all things' of Matthew 28:20, thus he saw many received into local assembly fellowship. In this booklet our brother has set out truth which we would heartily endorse, and commend for an unbiased consideration of 'things which are most surely believed among us'. As this edition goes to press may our beloved Lord bless its continued ministry to the generation of our day.

J. R. Baker

Contents

Reception to God's Assembly

W. Bunting

The subject of "reception" is one which from time to time has occasioned much discussion amongst the assemblies of God's people.

There are those who assert that we should welcome to the Lord's Supper all who profess the Name of Christ, whether or not they have manifested a desire to be obedient to the Word of God, as for instance, with regard to baptism; and this even though they may have no intention whatever of severing their unscriptural ecclesiastical associations. It is maintained that since the basis of fellowship is life in Christ, no one professing to have that life should be kept back from the Supper, provided that he or she is morally clean in life and doctrinally sound in what we call "The Fundamentals."

Those who advocate this view do not hesitate to declare that brethren who do otherwise are acting unscripturally and that their strictness is one of the present-day barriers to blessing in assemblies. They therefore call upon us to break down these barriers and to "open our doors, our arms, and our hearts to all God's children everywhere!'

In the following pages we give our reasons for dissenting from this view, together with a positive statement of what we believe Scripture teaches upon this vexed question. It is hoped that these may be used by the Lord to settle the minds of any of His beloved people who may be confused by the conflict of opinions upon the subject, and to establish them in an aspect of truth which ought to be "most surely believed among us."

PRELIMINARY REMARKS

Having regard, however, to certain unwise and mistaken ideas, the expressing of which only breeds misunderstanding and ill-will among Christians, it seems advisable to offer here a few preliminary remarks of a general character. In these we wish to make it clear that we are not ignorant of the

DANGER OF PHARISAISM AND SECTARIANISM

In the first place, we desire all to feel assured that we do not question the sincerity or godliness of others, because they differ from us upon the subject under consideration. Many in the past and present who have been staunch believers in what is known as "The Open Table" have been men of undoubted spirituality. We gladly acknowledge too, that outside of all assemblies there are numerous saints who are marked by deep devotion to the Lord, and whose personal piety and Gospel zeal put many of us to shame. To make lofty Church claims, as some do, and to imagine that '"we are the people" would be only to reveal a Laodicean spirit (see Rev. 3:17). God will blow upon all such human pretensions. The proud aloofness of the Pharisee is totally at variance with the precept and example of Christ (Lk. 18:11).

11

We humbly pray, therefore, that the perusal of this booklet will encourage no such conceit. Sectarianism, too, is hateful to Him "Who walketh in the midst of the seven golden lampstands." We do well to remember that while we may not occupy a sectarian position outwardly, there is ever the danger of harbouring a sectarian condition inwardly. The whole truth of God, therefore, should be held in equal balance, every part and doctrine of it having due weight upon our hearts. Our spiritual affections should embrace as much fellowship as is scripturally possible with all Christians, and be glad to welcome everyone whom the Word does not disqualify, while, of course, refusing everyone whom it does.

"We would remember we are one,
With every saint that loves Thy Name,
United to Thee on the Throne,
Our life, our hope, our Lord the same."

We heartily agree with the assertion that love is the supreme motive, and mainspring of the Christian life, but we would respectfully remind those who seem to play continually upon this one string, that love "rejoiceth in the truth" (1 Cor. 13:6), and "this is the love of God, that we keep His commandments" (1 Jn. 5:3). Love for all saints, does not mean love for all sects. Let us not make the mistake of thinking that the separation enjoined in such passages as Rom. 16:17; 2 Cor. 6: 14-18; Eph. 5:11; 2 Thess. 3:6; 2 Tim. 3:5; Heb. 13:13; and Rev. 18:4 is sectarianism. Rather it is obedience to the explicit teaching of God's Word, as is the caution in reception to fellowship seen in Acts 9:26; 2 John 10. Slackness in both these matters which is so characteristic a feature in many quarters to-day, is surely prejudicial to, and destructive of, corporate testimony. We observe with deep regret that many seem to have no clear apprehension of the fact that the very existence of assemblies signifies a Scriptural protest against sectarianism. The movement first established itself in the simple commemoration of our Lord's death each first day of the week; and as more and more light broke forth from the Word of God, its separation from the humanly devised and organised systems of religion became correspondingly more pronounced. It was a return to the simplicity of first principles, in which respect it was vitally different from later movements. Isn't it rather ironical that those who intermingle with the denominations and thus help to build up sectarianism, are the very ones who view as "sectarian" their brethren, whose only offence is that they desire at all costs to adhere loyally to those first principles?

DANGER OF HUMAN RULES

In our zeal to conform faithfully to these first principles, however, we must always guard against the danger of human rules not found in the Word at all. There is ever the tendency to go from one extreme to another. Therefore in the matter of reception, we must not forge cast-iron laws which the Scriptures do not warrant. Each applicant for assembly fellowship should be taken upon his or her own personal merits. A manifest willingness to bow obediently to God's Word is the one great requirement. We are not authorised to extract a pledge which would make one feel in bondage to human authority. Another has well said that "this would only hinder 'the obedience of faith,' which can never go beyond the measure of the enlightenment given by the Spirit of God." "I would certainly refuse,"* wrote the late Mr. Wm. Rodgers, "to be bound by a Medo-Persian law that none may ever, in any circumstances, be received, unless he or she first submit to baptism. To take that stand would constitute us a sect of Baptists, and this of the 'strictest' kind. Indeed one might as readily hold that baptism should be refused to any believer, unless he will undertake to come into the assembly immediately afterwards."

The enforcing of human rules in assembly life may maintain order and may appear practicable for a time, but it is legalistic, and requires no spirituality to carry it on. It flourishes even where carnality and worldliness abound. Usually it is characterised by a harsh and hypercritical attitude towards Christians not in the same circle. This certainly is not of God, and sooner or later it leads to the most disastrous consequences, as has been proven again and again. We must confess to our shame that not a few godly souls have been turned away from assemblies by the uncharitable treatment which they received. It is impossible to maintain a true testimony without the conscious presence of God. No rules, scriptural or otherwise, can take the place of this. Indeed it could be forfeited, even while we are clinging tenaciously to those precious basic words "Where two or three are gathered together in my name, there am I in the midst of them" (Matt. 18:20). It is very possible to continue with the form and formula and to have a name to live while dead cf (Rev. 3:1; Jer. 7:4). The very barrenness and hardness of our meetings would thus make our claim to His presence sadly but clearly untrue (Josh. 7:12). **It cannot be emphasised too often that scriptural principles require spiritual power if they are to function effectively**. When we experience weakness and failure, however, let us never imagine that a desire to act strictly in accordance with Scripture is equivalent to making rules.

See explanatory reference to this statement on page 18/19.

OUR REASONS

We shall now proceed to state our reasons for dissenting from the Open Table view.

1. THE CASE OF A STRANGER

The person desiring to break bread may be a complete stranger, or at least but little known, to the saints with whom he/she wishes to remember the Lord. In the brief time which elders usually have to interview such a one before the meeting begins, it is not reasonable to expect them to make sure of the visitor being really one of Christ's and of there being no cause for refusing fellowship. In the case of a complete stranger, full investigation would be well nigh impossible. This being so, the principle, "Lay hands hastily on no man" (1 Tim. 5:22, R.V.), should surely govern their attitude towards him. It may be objected that this verse has no reference to assembly reception. Primarily that is true, but the principle of caution which it lays down in connection with the appointing of elders, is surely of wider application. It was because the saints of the Jerusalem assembly acted upon this principle, in Acts 9:26, that Saul was not free to walk in and take his place among them without a question being asked. Moreover, the fact that visiting Christians in apostolic times were expected to bring with them letters of commendation (Rom. 16:1-2; 2 Cor. 3:1, etc.) is further proof that care in the reception of strangers was then necessary. How much more is it necessary now! In those days there were no apostate sects. Should we act as though there were none today? At that time so much of the Divine presence and power was realised in assemblies, and identification therewith called forth such reproach and opposition from the world, that few, comparatively speaking, who were not truly born again, ventured to apply for reception. "And of the rest durst no man join himself to them" (Acts 5:13). It was somewhat the same a century ago when assemblies, as we know them now, were formed. Today, however, apostolic power and discernment is conspicuously absent. Profession of the name of Christ is easy and in many cases popular, and the world's frown is seldom seen. Not only so, but the "last days," marked by increasing evils and imposture, heresies and apostasy, as foretold in Scripture, are upon us. Are watchfulness, discernment, and faithfulness in dealing with strangers not therefore needed more than ever?

Even if the visitor be known to some in the assembly and they vouch for him/her being a Christian, other members of the company, who at the opening of the meeting have no opportunity to express their minds, may know facts regarding the visitor which are quite sufficient to warrant rejection. What must be the feeling of such when they see this one brought in? Their consciences will be wounded. They will possibly be stumbled. At any rate the assembly will be no longer "joined together in the same mind and in the same judgement" (1 Cor. 1:10). Further, the Spirit will be grieved, and consequently the very object of their coming together will more or less be hindered. Indeed, the ultimate outcome may be division in the assembly.

We would here suggest the advisability of at least

two elders being at the hall early enough on the Lord's Day mornings, to meet possible visitors, and not just a few minutes before the meeting is due to commence, as is sometimes the case.

2. INVITING FRIENDS

In such instances it is only because of friends inviting them that such persons wish to partake of the Supper. There has been little or no exercise of soul on their part about obedience to the Word, no real conviction inwrought by the Holy Spirit that this is "the commandment of the Lord." They "break bread" merely as a gesture of Christian courtesy, or as a matter of convenience for the time being. What they do is not the fruit of heart subjection to "the knowledge of His will," for if it were they would come to remain. How can service of this kind be acceptable to the Lord? Should not such be allowed to "occupy the room of the unlearned" (1 Cor. 14:16) until they have been instructed in "the way of God more perfectly"? It is to be regretted that some, when they are not allowed to partake of the memorials of the Lord's death, feel disappointed and slighted, and consequently never come back. We do not blame them so much as we blame those who brought them along, without giving them a simple explanation as to the order of the meeting. It is not easy, however, to understand the attitude or mentality of one who, apart from the mere wish to be courteous, comes along with deliberate purpose to break bread once, and then return to the sect to which he or she belongs. Dealing with such a case as this, Wm. Rodgers well said: "The very existence of an assembly is a testimony that sectarianism and clericalism are wrong. On the other hand, if the sects and their clerics are right, the assembly must be entirely wrong. Why then should any conscientious person, who believes his own sect to be right and scriptural, wish to join himself, even for once, with a company which, according to his view, is quite in the wrong? If, however, he has discovered that it is the assembly that is in the right, then his sect must be wrong and why should he purpose to return to it? There are perhaps two other possibilities. He may not be very particular as to whether he is doing right or wrong. If so, observing without partaking is the most fitting place for him, until his conscience becomes exercised. On the other hand, he maybe in doubt as to which thing is right and which is wrong. In that case he will surely prefer to remain an onlooker, until such time as he sees clearly that what is being practised there is according to the Scriptures."

With reference to those who invite them, one may ask, what will be the result if all in the assembly seek to exercise the same privilege? "A queer kettle of fish we shall have," as the late Mr. W.J. McClure once remarked when speaking on this subject. Before long confusion would take the place of rule and order in God's assembly.

"If one exercises this supposed privilege," wrote the late Mr. J.R. Caldwell, "then others will do the same, and either godly oversight is entirely set aside, or else this liberty is granted to some and denied to others, thus raising most invidious and unscriptural distinctions. The result of this independent action is to constitute two circles of fellowship, called 'permanent' and 'occasional'. Or, if the unscripturalness of such a distinction be seen, and all who are brought in to 'break bread' are regarded as in fellowship, then there are those 'in fellowship' of whom the assembly knows nothing, concerning whom those having oversight have exercised no care and no discernment. In most cases, they are allowed to come and go as they please, thereby being a constant source of weakness and stumbling to those who are truly exercised before God."

We would not wish to be uncharitable, but we feel that those who contend most strongly for the right to bring their Christian friends to sit with them at the Lord's Supper, are usually those who are most prone to attend meetings in various denominational circles, and who brook no restraint or counsel in this direction, but are a law unto themselves.

It may be argued, however, that in Acts 9 Saul was received by the Jerusalem assembly upon the testimony of one man - Barnabas. That is true, but let us consider the full facts. We are told that Saul "essayed to join (i.e. to adhere to, or to identify with) himself to the disciples." Thus this was not at all a case of being invited by a friend. Saul himself took the initiative, and this he did knowing that bitter persecution awaited him. At first the disciples "were all afraid of him, and believed not that he was a disciple" (v. 26). Then Barnabas took up his case. He "brought him to the apostles" and testified to them of his conversion and subsequent life, which, of course, would include the fact that as a believer he had been baptized. Saul was then made welcome to full fellowship. From this it seems perfectly clear that before the young convert was received, there was ample time for all the saints as well as the apostles, to satisfy themselves unitedly that he was a genuine believer; and his conduct afterwards did not disappoint them, for he was with them "coming in and going out at Jerusalem!' **It requires to be emphasised that it is the whole Church that receives fellow saints, and not just the elders.** In view of this we commend the practice of announcing the name of the applicant to the whole assembly a week or so in advance, and giving the right to anyone in fellowship to lodge an objection, or have a conversation with the candidate, in the intervening period.

3. OCCASIONAL FELLOWSHIP

When we appeal to the Scriptures we find in them no precedent whatever for "occasional fellowship." Never in Acts, which covers the first 30 years of Church history, nor in the Epistles, do we read of such a thing. What we do read is that "they continued steadfastly … in breaking of bread" (Acts 2:42), and that Saul, after being brought into the assembly in Jerusalem, "was with them coming in and going out" (Acts 9:28). Such reception is "as Christ also received us," and "to the glory of God" (Rom. 15:7). To receive those who attend as occasion suits, possibly because they are on holiday and far away from home, and then return to their own particular sect, to support principles which are entirely opposite to those of the assembly, is neither the one nor the other. Indeed, we may be permitted to express wonder why it is so urgently important that they should join in the Breaking of Bread on perhaps one Lord's Day of the year, while they can get on without this during the other fifty-one. No doubt, in isolated cases, Christians thus received have been so impressed by the scriptural simplicity of the meeting that they never returned to the denomination with which they were formerly associated. This, however, in no way proves that "occasional fellowship" is right. Many could testify that they were as much impressed while only observing, as if they had been actually partaking of the Supper. Anyhow, our guide as to church order is the Word of God, and not the varying experiences of His people.

Moreover, the practise of thus receiving professing Christians means that in the assembly there are not only two kinds of reception, but also two circles of communion - an inner and an outer - known, as we have already seen, as "permanent fellowship" and "occasional fellowship." We have read of one assembly the roll of which was divided into two columns under these respective heads. In another, a believer who had been a casual participant at the Breaking of Bread for some months, was not invited to the annual assembly Tea meeting, since it was only for those in "permanent fellowship." Now, such distinctions are not in harmony with the plain teaching of the Epistles, especially 1 Corinthians, where Paul insists so strongly upon assembly unity. In addition, they are likely to lead to serious complications. For instance, if after being in this outer circle for a time the individual concerned does not decide to enter full fellowship, is he to continue indefinitely to exercise the privilege of "breaking bread" at such times as he pleases, or must he suffer the embarrassment of being asked to refrain from partaking of the Lord's Supper? If he falls into open sin, how would discipline be carried out? From what is he to be "put away"? (1 Cor. 5:13). Further, in the event of another person having to be put away, how can he share in the exercise of such discipline? Again, supposing a Christian from the denomination to which our visitor nominally belongs is being received into full and happy fellowship, how can he participate in the reception? "Occasional fellowship" may sound well in theory, but when reduced to practice it is absurd, for it means that in the assembly there are two classes - one that has power to function governmentally in accordance with Scripture, and another that cannot possibly share in such responsibility.

"We candidly confess," wrote Mr John Ritchie, the first Editor of "The Believers' Magazine," "that, notwithstanding all the reasonings and arguments that are advanced to justify 'occasional reception,' we have never yet seen a vestige of Scripture to guide in it - that is, to justify inviting those concerning whose doctrine and conduct very little can be known, to share in part of a fellowship which they have no heart for, or knowledge of, and which but for the invitation of friends, they never would have thought of patronizing at all."

4. QUESTIONABLE TEACHING

In the various denominations there are many Christians who on matters of importance hold doctrines and theories which we believe to be unscriptural. We think for instance of some who teach that a born again person may fall away and be eventually lost; of some who deny the eternal Sonship of Christ; of those who believe in speaking in tongues as a sign of the Baptism of the Spirit; of those who claim to be entirely sanctified and able to live without sin; of many who contend for women having equal right with men to preach in public, to mention but a few unscriptural issues. Most clergymen practise Infant Sprinkling, solemnly declaring (according to the book from which they read) that an infant at its "baptism" is made "a member of Christ, a child of God, and an inheritor of the kingdom of Heaven" - which unquestionably is a Romish and soul destroying doctrine. It is a little consolation to know that some do not at heart believe the words of this formula. Such, however, could not be expected to minister the Word to the edification of scripturally baptized believers. Yet if they are free to break bread when they please may they not take advantage of the liberty for ministry which obtains in our meetings to express their views there? We cannot very well bring a man into the circle of fellowship and at the same time impose upon him a ban against speaking what he believes. If, therefore, some from the above-mentioned groups come along and teach their peculiar tenets, or if a woman gets up to instruct the saints, contrary to the plain prohibition of 1 Tim. 2:12, what terrible confusion and unrest must ensue! "God is not the author of confusion but peace, as in all the churches of the saints" (1 Cor. 14:33). Whether or not such a contingency should arise, this kind of reception is tantamount to leaving the door of the assembly open to teaching of a questionable character, and God, who is zealous for His Truth, will not approve of such laxity. If "a little leaven leaveneth the whole lump" (Gal. 5:9), no taint of it would He wish to be mixed with His children's food. One thinks of many Scriptures that express Divine impatience with teaching which unsettles saints and causes the simple to err from the truth. Therefore elders are responsible to see to it, that so far as lies in their power, the door of the assembly is closed against it.

Dealing with the question of whether unbaptized believers should be received at the Lord's Supper. Mr. Andrew Borland. M.A.. has said the following, which illustrates the importance of this. The practice alluded to "opens the door," he writes. "for an unbaptized believer in an assembly to propagate privately, and probably to teach publicly. what he believes. If a gifted brother holding such views is not at liberty to teach. then the situation becomes ludicrous. for restrictions are put upon his fellowship. Should such get into positions of leadership in the assembly, it is possible to imagine a time, not very far removed, when the truth would cease to be taught and practised. How dangerous to open the door to such a possibility! Is it not better to adhere rigidly to the method of the New Testament?" Our brother further says of this practice: "It tends to shut the mouths of ministering brethren who agree to admit such, a person. How can they teach baptism to others when they are willing to dispense with its necessity in the case of some? Ministry along these lines would be a self-condemnation." Let it be understood that there is no contradiction between

25

this statement and that by Mr. Rodgers upon an earlier page, condemning the view that "none may ever in any circumstance be received unless he or she first submit to baptism." Mr. Rodgers has in mind a believer who manifests a willingness to obey what he finds in the Word, but is in peculiar circumstances, because of say, some physical disability. Mr Borland is thinking of a person who consistently repudiates immersion, and is likely to propagate his views in the assembly, if received.

5. RECEPTION ALWAYS TO THE ASSEMBLY

Not only has Scripture nothing to say about "occasional fellowship", but it never speaks of reception to the Lord's Supper at all. This may sound strange, yet it is true, for though the New Testament presents various aspects of reception, it has nothing to say about receiving to the Breaking of Bread as we noted earlier. **What the Scripture teaches is reception to the fellowship of the assembly,** to share its privileges and responsibilities, its joys and sorrows. The Worship or Remembrance Meeting is but one of its many activities, as we see in Acts 2:41,42. Visiting Christians, in apostolic times, were received not merely to the Lord's Supper, but to the fellowship of the assembly. See Acts 15:4; Rom. 16:1; 3 John 9. Some may enquire, "But why are letters of commendation always read at the Morning Meeting and names announced then, if you don't receive to the Lord's Supper?" Our simple two-fold answer is this: firstly, it is then that most saints are able to be present; secondly, this meeting is the highest expression of fellowship. Again it may be asked: "What about Rom. 15:7, 'Wherefore receive ye one another, as Christ also received us to the glory of God'? We reply that if its entire context be read, it will be seen that it makes no allusion whatever to the Remembrance Meeting. Since verses 5 and 6 contain a prayer for those already in assembly fellowship, that they may be "of the same mind one with another," so "that with one accord they may with one mouth glorify the God and Father of our Lord Jesus Christ" (R.V.), the injunction, "receive ye one another," can have no reference to the initial act of reception. It is simply an appeal, as the Old Testament quotations which immediately follow show, to the Jewish and Gentile sections of the Church at Rome to foster amongst themselves a warmer social and spiritual intercourse, and not to allow such matters as the observing of days and eating of certain meats (chap.14), to keep them more or less estranged from each other. "The Scripture," says Mr. Borland, "has no reference directly to the church, but to 'domestic fellowship'," while Mr. T.W. Ball, B.A., writes as follows: "This injunction has nothing to do with reception to an assembly, but as the wording makes plain, refers to the mutual receiving of Christians already enjoying assembly privileges. The initial reception to a local company is, allowed for in the words of chap. 14:1, 'Him that is weak in the faith receive ye.' A sample of that which affects visitors and migrants is seen in chap. 16:1 in the case of Phoebe. The facts of her identification with the assembly at Cenchrea is stated as making it possible for the saints at Rome to 'receive her in the Lord'."

Even if this passage did refer to the initial act of assembly reception, however, a careful reading of it will show clearly that it could only mean reception to the full and permanent fellowship of the church. The exhortation, **"receive ye one another",** would surely indicate that reception is to be mutual. The assembly is to welcome to its fellowship the candidate, and the candidate is to welcome to his confidence and affections the assembly with its privileges and responsibilities. In a word, the fellowship is to be full and reciprocal. It was thus that **"Christ also received us".** There surely was nothing temporary, or "occasional," or one-sided about that reception? He welcomed us in all our need, and we in the same joyful moment accepted Him as our Saviour. Thus we became one forever. Reception to church fellowship after this pattern would be "to the glory of God" but open reception, which knows nothing of reciprocity and carries with it no sense of responsibility, is neither after the pattern of Christ's welcoming us, nor is it **"to the glory of God".**

The expression in Rom. 16:1, "in the Lord", above referred to is one which oft recurs in the New Testament. It reminds us of the solemn fact, which cannot be impressed too deeply upon our minds, viz., that the assembly is a sphere in which the Lordship of Christ is recognised. All that is carried on should be in absolute harmony with it. Everything that obscures or overthrows this truth should be vetoed. No-one can deny this who agrees that the precept of Rom. 13:14: "Put ye on the Lord Jesus Christ, and make no provision for *the flesh," is* both a valid and valuable principle for the assembly.

FALLACIES

There are a few popular fallacies which we must now examine:

THE ASSEMBLY AS A FAMILY

There are those who speak of the assembly as a family, and their maxim is, "The Father's Table is for all His children." They teach that life, not light, is the basis of fellowship, that reception should be simple and informal, like welcoming a newborn infant to the family circle, and that the only examination which Scripture enjoins is that of 1 Cor. 11:28: "Let a man examine **himself** and so let him eat."

Is the assembly, however, compared with a family in God's Word? In answer to this question, Dr. Rowland Edwards, Australia, writes: "Metaphors and designations of the local church abound - but among them that of the family is conspicuous by its absence... Despite the fact that nothing is commoner among mankind than the family, reception to the local church is never compared with the entry of a newly born child into a family." We heartily agree, and would add that it is a great mistake to speak of the Father's table as though it were synonymous with the Lord's table. The former term never occurs in the New Testament, but it is implied in the story of the prodigal in Luke 15. We are introduced to it immediately at conversion. It symbolizes the rich feast which grace has provided for us in salvation. Though backsliding may temporarily mar our enjoyment of it, no power can rob us of a place at our Father's table.

On the other hand, our participating of the Lord's

Table is contingent upon our obedience and our separation from evil (1 Cor. 10:21). The one feast is figurative and continuous, the other is literal and is celebrated each Lord's Day.

It is clear to readers, we hope, that the word "table" in this passage does not stand merely for the material of the piece of furniture upon which the emblems, bread and cup, are placed. The use of the word here is an illustration of that figure of speech named metonymy, by which the name of a thing is placed for that of another closely related to it. Thus "the cup" (1 Cor. 10:16; 11:28) means that which is in the cup. "The table of the Lord," accordingly, signifies the privileges and spiritual provisions and blessings, in which those who partake at the table share.

As for the contention that life, not light, is the basis of fellowship, we would point out that life and light are inseparable. Every born again soul has some measure of light. "They shall be all taught of God"' (John 6:45); and "the anointing which ye have received of him ... teacheth you all things" (1 John 2:27). How are we to know that an applicant for reception has divine life, if he is unable to answer some simple questions which will reveal what light he possesses? Of course, to insist upon full knowledge to begin with, would be, as T.W Ball has aptly said, "as foolish as expecting the wisdom of a man from an infant."

All one requires to say about 1 Cor. 11:28 is that is has absolutely nothing to do with reception. It is an injunction to those already enjoying assembly fellowship to search their hearts before coming to the Remembrance Meeting, lest some unjudged sin might hinder their communion and worship.

NON-SINFUL THINGS

It is taught by some that no one should be requested to give up any non-sinful thing in order to be eligible for church fellowship. This sounds very feasible, but how are we to determine what is sinful and what is not? Where are we to draw the line? Is it not sinful to spend the Lord's time playing worldly games, to go joy-riding on the Lord's Day, or to participate in the world's politics? Supposing a candidate claims that his smoking and cinema-going are non-sinful, must the assembly receive him? This would be very accommodating for carnal professors. We certainly would not refuse a man fellowship merely because he played a game, or in a moment of weakness smoked. If a man, however, refused to part with practices which belong to the natural man, because he loved them or was powerless to relinquish them, we would seriously doubt if he knew the Lord at all. Upon that ground we believe he should be refused assembly fellowship. The Lord Jesus said, "Why call ye Me, Lord, Lord, and do not the things which I say?" (Lk. 6:46). Again, Paul wrote, "If any man be in Christ he is a new creature" (creation) (2 Cor. 5:17). If a candidate contends that he knows some in fellowship who are doing questionable things, enquiry should at once be made as to the truth of his allegation.

ARGUMENTS BASED UPON SILENCE

Another fallacy is that of basing an argument upon the silence of Scripture.

THE EUNUCH

It is contended, for instance, that baptism is not essential for reception to the local church, but that faith in Christ alone is. As proof of this we are told, that "the eunuch was baptized, but we never read of his being in a local church. He may have been, but the silence of Scripture on this point is instructive." What instruction this silence affords us, it is hard to see. To be candid, it teaches us nothing. We might as well conclude that the Ethiopian never again read the book of Isaiah, never afterwards prayed nor witnessed for Christ, because Acts 8 does not expressly say that he did these things.

THE CASE OF APOLLOS

An attempt to prove the same thing is also made from the fact that in Acts 18 Luke does not say that Apollos, who "knew only the baptism of John" (v.25), was baptized with Christian baptism before being received by Aquila and Priscilla, in whose house the church met (1 Cor. 16:19). From this it is suggested that strangers, even though they hold questionable teaching, should be received to assembly fellowship and later instructed in the truth.

Is there ground, however, for concluding that Apollos was not baptized just because it is not mentioned that he was? "Are we to imagine," asks Dr. Edwards, "that the Christians at Antioch in Syria were not baptized because the narrative of the formation and early growth of this assembly omits mention of it? Was not baptism universal among Christians then?" There is another possible explanation of this silence, however. It may be that

Apollos had been baptized with John's baptism, while it was still valid - before it was superseded by Christian baptism - in which case he probably did not require to be re-baptized. The apostles were disciples of John, and there is no record of their being baptized again.

Regarding the statement that the church met in the house of Aquila and Priscilla, this does not necessarily imply that the clause, "they took him unto them" (v.26), means that they received him into assembly fellowship. Surely such receiving does not fall within the province of a sister or a man and his wife. Clearly what the verse means is that Aquila and Priscilla took Apollos to their home, showed him hospitality, as they were accustomed to do with strangers (see Acts 18:1-3; Rom. 16:3,4), and "expounded unto him the way of God more perfectly." Can one imagine that their instruction did not include Christian Baptism, as one of the first steps of loving obedience to the Lord?

WAS THERE A CHURCH AT TROAS?

Again, since it is not anywhere recorded that there was a church at Troas, attempts are made to show that in Acts 20:5-12 the Apostle and his eight travelling companions broke bread upon their journey, where there was no permanent assembly testimony. The R.V. reading of verse 7, "when we were gathered together to break bread," is relied upon as supporting this view. If, however, the "we" refers exclusively to the Apostle and his party, how are we to understand the next clause, "Paul preached unto **them**"? Why does it not read, "Paul preached unto us"? Surely the reference here. and in v. 11, R.V. ("talked with **them** a long while"), and also in v. 12 (**"they** brought the young man alive") is to other saints who were also at the Lord's Supper. It seems superfluous to have to point this out. We are quite safe in concluding that there was an assembly at Troas, and that what is here described was the customary Remembrance Meeting upon the first day of the week. A reading of 2 Cor. 2:12, 13, leads to the same conclusion. It is there said of Paul at Troas that "taking his leave of them, he went from thence into Macedonia." From whom was he here parted? Was it not from the Lord's people? - of course it was.

It is therefore futile to appeal to Acts 20 as an example of brethren breaking bread where there was no assembly. The passage, however, does teach by example how often the Supper should be celebrated. "The custom of the church at Troas," wrote the late C.F. Hogg, "is recorded, surely, for our learning. The believers at Troas did not gather because Paul and his party were visiting them. On the contrary, the narrative plainly indicates that though the visitors arrived on the morning of Monday, and though their journey was urgent (v.16), yet they did not convene a special meeting for the purpose, but waited for the first day of the week." Let it be observed that Mr. Hogg, a most painstaking student of Scripture, did not hesitate to speak of "the church at Troas."

It is well to be warned that this principle of building an argument upon silence is one not infrequently used by Higher Critics in their attacks upon God's Word. To expose the fallacy of such a principle, Prof.

R.D. Wilson in his book, "Is the Higher Criticism Scholarly?" makes an interesting reference to Scribner's History of the United States of America. This work has 53 pages of Index, double column, in which the word "Presbyterian" never occurs, "Church" only twice, and "Christian" only in the phrase "Christian Commission." Further, in 3,500 pages quarto there is no mention of "Thanksgiving Day," and the Bible is referred to only in the relation of the Bible Society to slavery. Yet how foolish it would be to conclude from these silences that Christianity is practically unknown in the United States, and that the last Thursday of November is not set apart for the giving of thanks in that land! Thus while admittedly there is often significance in the silence of Scripture, it is, as Andrew Borland, M.A., recently wrote, "**a most dangerous procedure**" **to build an argument upon such a basis.**

ONLY ONE FELLOWSHIP

It has been taught that God recognises but one fellowship, that of His saints, and that, therefore, we should do likewise. Now it is true that all Christians have been "called unto the fellowship of His Son" (1 Cor. 1:9), know in varying measure the "communion (fellowship) of the Holy Spirit" (2 Cor. 13:14), and also know something of the aspects of fellowship of which Paul writes in his Epistle to the Philippians: (1) Fellowship in the Gospel (ch. 1:5); (2) Fellowship in the sufferings of Christ (ch. 3:10); and (3) Fellowship in sacrificial giving ("communicate," ch. 4:14). There is, however, a distinct and definite assembly fellowship, as the record of Acts 2:42 shows. This is conditioned jointly upon obedience to: (a) the call to separation in 2 Cor. 6: "What communion (fellowship) hath light with darkness?"; (b) the warning of 2 John, not to receive or help false teachers, otherwise one would be a "partaker (i.e. one who has fellowship) with their evil deeds"; and (c) the plain veto of Eph. 5: "Have no fellowship with the unfruitful works of darkness."

Now, if we have the Spirit's mind, we also shall acknowledge that there are various aspects of Christian fellowship. The pity is that there are those to-day who have no heart for some of them; and though we may love God's people with a deep affection, how can we meet for public testimony upon common ground with those who persist in treating certain parts of "the apostles' doctrine" as "non-essentials", except by a shameful compromise of truths vital to assembly life which our Lord has taught us?

Again, it is taught that all believers in a given district are in the church in that district, whether or not they gather according to Matt. 18:20. We believe that all saints are in "the Church, which is His Body, the fullness of Him that filleth all in all" (Eph. 1:22,23). The Epistles as plainly speak of another aspect, however, according to which the term refers to a company of saints, gathered in scriptural fellowship, as a testimony for the Lord, in a particular place. Thus we read of "the churches of God" (1 Cor. 11:16), and the "churches of the saints" (1 Cor. 14:33). This is a more restricted view, and in it all Christians in a district may not be embraced, though ideally and potentially they belong to it. For instance, in 1 Cor. 14:23 we read: "If, therefore THE WHOLE CHURCH be come together in one place ... and there come in those that are unlearned OR unbelievers..." The "unlearned" are here distinct from the "unbelievers", therefore they must be saints, yet they are not included in "the whole church". Compare 1 Cor. 5:13, where one who later proved himself to be a believer was to be "put away" from the church; and 3rd John 10, which speaks of godly souls being "cast out of the church."

It is a pity when we can see only one side of Divine truth. The result is ill-balanced ministry, and the present confusion about assembly reception is in large measure due to this. The singular thing is that those who are so straitened in their views are the very ones who complain about their brethren being "narrow." One could wish that such would put the shoe on the right foot. Let us all give heed to Paul's counsel to Timothy: "Study to shew thyself approved unto God, a workman that needeth not to be ashamed, rightly dividing the word of truth" (2 Tim. 2:15).

NO DEFINITE PATTERN

Many have the idea that there is no pattern given for us to follow in the New Testament. We have, therefore, to fall back upon expediency and ingenuity, and thus, like the Children of Israel in the time of the Judges "do every man that which is right in his own eyes" (Jud. 17:6). They agree, of course, that Moses had nothing left to his originality or imagination, when constructing the Tabernacle. The Lord said, "see that thou make all things according to the pattern showed to thee in the mount" (Heb. 8:5). That legislated for all measurements and materials. They were not to deviate a hairsbreadth. Now we must confess that we to-day have no such thing as mathematical details. As we have already pointed out more than once, we must not forge cast-iron rules. Surely, however. there are guiding, governing principles which eliminate the carnal wisdom of men.

The Book of Acts, and the subsequent Epistles, bear the imprint of the GREAT COMMISSION of Matt. 28: "Go and make disciples of all nations, baptizing them into the Name of the Father, and of the Son, and of the Holy Spirit, teaching them to observe all things whatsoever I have commanded you." The concluding words of Christ, "Lo, I am with you all the days, even unto the end of the world", show the universal and perpetual validity of His 'marching orders'. The very word which is translated "make disciples" in Matt. 28:19 is found in Acts 14:21, and rendered "taught many." Chapters 2 and 18 of Acts give the apostolic order:-

(a) The Gospel was boldly preached.
(b) Sinners repented and were forgiven.
(c) These obeyed the Lord in water-baptism by immersion.
(d) They were formed into assemblies or added thereto.
(e) Gifts were raised up by the Risen Head to shepherd them.

Thus "they continued stedfastly in the apostles'

doctrine, in fellowship, and in breaking of bread and in prayers" (ch.2:42). "Many of the Corinthians, hearing, believed and were baptized" (ch. 18:8), and were taught by the Apostle Paul according to the tenor of the two Epistles addressed to them. We read in Acts 17 of many souls being saved at Thessalonica. Paul later could thank God that these "became imitators (followers) of the churches of God which are in Judaea in Christ Jesus" (1 Thess. 2:14 R.V.).

If we have rightly discerned the mind of God in the New Testament, we cannot but see apostolic unanimity and uniformity in teaching and practice. Paul's words: "Even as I teach everywhere in every church" (1 Cor. 4:17), could have been written by all the twelve, for they did "all speak the same thing" (1 Cor. 1:10). Compare 2 Peter 3:15.

How far the denominations have departed from Divine principle and order should be obvious at a glance. Isn't it the general practice among them to-day, that upon attaining to a certain age, about 14-16 years, young people are urged to "join the Church." Special classes are arranged for them. Seldom, if ever, is any question asked about the vital experience of the grace of God in conversion. In fact such interrogation as, "**How, when** and **where** were you saved?" would be severely frowned upon. They generally excuse laxity by quoting Matt. 13:30: "Let both grow together until the harvest," wilfully ignoring Christ's own words of commentary, "the field is the world" -not the church (v. 38). Another refuge is Matt. 7:1, "Judge not, that ye be not judged" - which has to do only with Christians being censorious of each other. Are we to become like them in their careless, unscriptural ways? Rather let us adhere to the Divine pattern as found in the teaching and practice of the Apostles. That pattern has never been revised nor modified to suit the times, and neither the present divided state of the saints nor the fact that there have been good men who in practice did not comply with it, is any excuse for our departing therefrom.

LETTERS OF COMMENDATION

Many consider that there is no need to-day for these, but such passages as Acts 18:27; Rom. 16:1,2 and 2 Cor. 3:1 are not to be dispensed with. In accordance with them we believe that Christians visiting another assembly or taking up residence in a new district, should carry with them letters of commendation. These, we suggest, should in every case be dated and signed by at least two responsible brethren. This New Testament practice has a number of advantages. In the first place, it forms a happy link of fellowship between one assembly and another. This in itself is most desirable, for everything possible should be done to preserve and promote good relations among companies of the Lord's people. In the next place, it affords an opportunity of expressing the esteem in which the person concerned is held in the circle which he or she is leaving. Of this we have a fine example in Rom. 16:1,2. Every person, of course, should not be given the same commendation. Some are more worthy than others. For this reason the use of stereotyped, printed forms, which in some quarters have become popular in recent years, is not to be recommended. A letter of introduction also ensures a believer of the confidence of the saints to whom he or she is going, and of a ready welcome to their fellowship and hospitality and such assistance as they may be in a position to render.

Further, this practise eases the burden of responsibility which devolves upon elders. It saves questioning and in some cases embarrassment, at the beginning of the Remembrance Supper, when our minds should be as free as possible from care and distraction.

Not only so, but the use of letters of commendation is a safeguard against the danger of one who has been in trouble in his home assembly, or who may even have been excommunicated therefrom on account of evil, being received in another company of believers. Mr. WE Vine, M.A., in his work, "The Church and the Churches", has well said: "Due care on the part of the spiritual guides in the churches should be sufficient to obviate the intrusion of one under discipline into any particular assembly. Let a note of commendation be required. For such a person to go off and seek the fellowship of another assembly and there to be received, is to ignore the authority of Christ, and to contravene the unity of the Spirit, which we are enjoined to endeavour to keep (Eph. 4:3). An act of church discipline is not simply the act of the assembly, when rightly used it is the exercise of the authority of Christ carried out in His Name and power (1 Cor. 5:4). The realisation of that is itself sufficient to enforce the solemn and binding character of the discipline."

Lastly, let it be said that elders assume a grave responsibility before God, if they refuse a letter of commendation to a saint with whom they have, for years perhaps, been breaking bread, unless there is a very solid and satisfactory reason for so doing. Yet instances of the most unkind and unjust refusals have, alas, not been unknown in assembly experience.

SERVANTS OF CHRIST

In the case of a well known servant of Christ, of course, a letter of commendation should not be necessary. "Need we, as some others, epistles of commendation to you?" A solemn importance attaches to one's going forth for the first time, however, either to minister to saints or serve in the Gospel at home or abroad. This step should not be taken lightly or without the fellowship of one's own assembly, as Acts 13:3; 14:26; 15:40, and other passages, would indicate. Though an Apostle, called and commissioned directly by the Risen Lord, and in no way relying upon man, as we learn from Gal. 1:12-16, Paul did not move independently of his brethren, as Luke is careful to record. To him their fellowship was obviously a cherished possession. Acts 16:2 and 1 Tim. 4:14 imply the same thing with regard to Timothy. In the case, therefore, of one going forth for the first time, as also in that of a labouring brother visiting distant assemblies where he is unknown by face, it is advisable and indeed essential, that one should carry a letter expressing the approval and fellowship of one's home assembly.

In the giving of letters godly care should be

exercised. "Plainly", says Mr. C.F. Hogg, "if those who give commendatory letters to preachers and teachers do not exercise due care in seeing that those upon whom they thus lay hands are worthy in character and fitted for the work they undertake to do, much harm will accrue to the saints and to the testimony generally, and such letters will cease to have any value; and those given after a godly sort and to worthy persons will come under suspicion... Amiability, reluctance to give offence, amenability to flattery, the fear of man, and suchlike considerations too often account for commendations given to persons of questionable suitability, or even of obvious unsuitability for the service in view. `The thing that ye do is not good: ought ye not to walk in the fear of our Cod?` (Neh. 5:9). On the other hand, it would be a most serious matter to refuse a godly brother a letter just because of some personal dislike or petty disagreement. How deeply important it is, therefore, that in this matter elders in assemblies should, as Mr. Hogg further says, "preserve their consciences 'void of offence toward God and man always'."

It should be borne in mind, of course, that a letter is not a kind of certificate of membership which ensures that the bearer must be received. Brethren may know facts about such a one which will render his commendation absolutely valueless.

THE SERVANT'S RESPONSIBILITY

It should also be borne in mind, however, that when a brother goes forth in fellowship with his home assembly, he is thereafter directly responsible to the Lord alone for guidance as to his movements. A wise, godly brother, of course, will ever seek to act in a manner which will commend itself to the spiritually minded, and he will thus retain their confidence. At the same time it should ever be remembered that the worker is GOD'S servant, not man's. This is of paramount importance, and never should be lost sight of. Nothing should be allowed to obtrude between the godly, exercised servant and his Master. "For," said Paul, "if I yet pleased men, I should not be the servant of Christ" (Gal. 1:10).

"WE OUGHT TO RECEIVE SUCH"

Recognising this, it is our responsibility as well as our privilege to receive and assist all such. They are those honourable in life and sound in the faith. "For his name's sake they went forth, taking nothing of the Gentiles. We therefore ought to receive such, that we might be fellow helpers to the truth" (3 John 7:8). In his 2nd Epistle, John has told us the type of preacher we **are not to receive,** and to whom we are not to extend even a greeting (vs.10,11). Regarding this there must be no laxity in our day of numerous false cults and teaching which is subversive of the Gospel and of the right ways of the Lord. Unsound teachers are to be rejected. John, however, preserves a balance, for here in his 3rd Epistle he enjoins upon us that the true, genuine servant of God is **not to be rejected**. He is to be received. By way of warning, this is immediately followed by the account of a man - Diotrephes - who would not receive John nor other good brethren in whom John had confidence. If the beloved Apostle and his companions had yielded their God-given liberty and sacrificed a good conscience, in deference to the "preeminence" of Diotrephes, the door to the church would have been open to them. They, of course, would not do so, and the issue became so serious that those who "would" have received them were "cast out of the church". In other words, the issue led to open division in the assembly, which is a most serious matter.

It should be clear therefore that it would be a grave wrong to refuse a seat at the Lord's Supper to any visiting servant of Christ, who is in assembly fellowship, and whose life and doctrine are pure. It is the sin of Diotrephes. To exclude such is tantamount to relegating him to the place of the spiritually unclean leper, and so, outside assembly fellowship. Now, 1 Cor. 5:11 furnishes us with samples of the evil practices for which one should be excommunicated. Asked if it would be in order for a person to be put away from the fellowship of an assembly for "persistently attending meetings not conducted on scriptural lines", W. Rodgers replied "It would be quite wrong... to take such a step... The evil practices for which the guilty one should be put away from the Assembly are of a very different nature, being indeed such as would be accounted discreditable even amongst unsaved people. If saints were to be put away for causes such as those in the question, there probably would have been few left in the Corinthian assembly, since many of them were accepting invitations to the feasts of unbelievers (1 Cor. 10:27), and some appear to have been seen seated in idol temples (1 Cor. 8:10).

The Apostle deals with, and rebukes these and other similar practices, but he does not order that all concerned be swept out of the Meeting."

That what we have here been seeking to inculcate is not irrelevant or superfluous, the following cases will illustrate.

TWO ILLUSTRATIONS

A few years ago a well known speaker, who had held a high and responsible government post during the last war, and who was nominally in assembly fellowship, was announced to be the special preacher at a Sunday evening service in one of the major denominations in a certain town. To the surprise of the brethren in a near-by assembly, this brother presented himself for fellowship at the Remembrance Meeting that morning. What were the elders to do? They had not long to decide the matter. They informed the visitor that as they knew he was in assembly fellowship, he certainly would be received, but as the saints were grieved because of his sectarian association in their town, ministry by him would not be acceptable to many of them. Not feeling happy because of the obvious embarrassment of the brethren and the suggested restriction, the visitor withdrew without causing any further fuss or trouble. The decision of the elders, we believe, was balanced - graceful yet faithful, sane and scriptural.

Very different, however, is the second illustration. A missionary, also well known, and beloved for his life of devoted, sacrificial service, and adherence to assembly principles, remained for a time in a certain city, not many years ago. He felt it was the Lord's will that he should spend a Lord's Day with the saints of a particular assembly while there. The preceding Sundays, however, he had spent with adjacent assemblies, with which the one he now intended to visit was not, sad to relate, in fellowship. What was the result? When our brother came to the Remembrance Meeting, a very distressing situation revealed itself. He was not invited to the circle of fellowship, and after consultation the elders, not being agreed that he should be invited, allowed him to sit back in one of the seats usually occupied by the unconverted, the untaught, or those under assembly discipline. Had he apologized for having visited the neighbouring assemblies and given a promise that he would not return to them, possibly he would have been received with open arms. Another preacher known to the writer, when placed in very similar circumstances, did so, and was not debarred from fellowship. Yet when subsequently questioned, he acknowledged that he knew not of any unsoundness or unjudged sin in the other assembly he had visited. Our missionary brother, however, could not do this. His conscience would not allow him. Mean compliance with the unreasonable and unspiritual attitude manifested, would have been gross insincerity and dishonesty on his part, and would have reduced him, a servant of our Lord Jesus Christ, to the role of a mere time-server. Whether or not he was right in having fellowship with the other assemblies, it is not for us to say. He was the Lord's servant. It was no sect or interdenominational mission that he had visited, but scripturally gathered companies of saints. The only point we wish to make is that the brother was very wrongly treated. It is well, as these pages advocate, that responsible brethren should be cautious in reception. It is possible, however, to be righteous above what is written, to have zeal without knowledge, and to play the part of a cruel Diotrephes while ostensibly safeguarding the honour of the Lord.

To conclude, in the one case we have cited the elders acted scripturally, for they had no just ground for excluding the visitor; in the other, those responsible treated an honoured servant of God as though he had been in the same category as the wicked, incestuous man of 1 Cor. 5, and did so summarily, without the saints of the assembly having any voice in the matter. Indeed many of them were deeply grieved when they learned what had taken place. If this were an isolated case, it would not be so serious, but to the writer's knowledge the same thing has happened on other occasions as well. The record of all such high-handed, arbitrary action is with God, and has yet to be faced by those responsible at His solemn Judgment Seat.

SUGGESTIONS

To conclude, let us make a few suggestions worthy of consideration by God's people who are in assembly fellowship.

LOYALTY AND LOVE

We should be loyal to our assembly, giving it our undivided interest, seeking in every way possible to promote its spiritual well-being, and carefully avoiding any action which may mar its harmony. The self-will of some, under the guise of tolerance and love, in frequenting sectarian places, from which the assembly as a whole should be separated, is a constant source of grief and weakness to the saints with whom they are professedly in church fellowship.

Let us therefore "hold fast the form of sound words" (2 Tim. 1:13), and seek to "adorn the doctrine of God our Saviour in all things" (Tit. 2:10). Let us at the same time studiously avoid every expression of ridicule, or that which is calculated to "cut off ears", and let us manifest such a loving disposition to all saints that it never can truthfully be said of us that we are formal, proud, self-satisfied, or worldly. Then the testimony borne concerning us will be that "God is in them of a truth" (1 Cor. 14:25).

We should see to it that when believers are received, their reception is the warm, hearty act of all. Moreover, we should cultivate a spiritual atmosphere and an interesting, Christ exalting ministry in our meetings. Thus assemblies will have an attraction for Christians who are wearied of the unscriptural practices of the denominations. Of Asa it is written, "They fell to him out of Israel in abundance when they saw that the Lord his God was with him" (2 Chron. 15:9).

WISE AND GODLY ELDERS

We should pray that God will raise up in the assemblies elders who are "vigilant" (1 Tim. 3:2), men of wise judgment, godly care, and spiritual insight, who know what it is to stand in the counsel of the Lord. Such elders will be careful to ascertain if the motives which actuate applicants are pure. They will be on their guard against the devious and underhand methods sometimes adopted by folks to get their friends into assemblies. They will not give questionable young converts - not even the children of Christian parents, the benefit of the doubt, and receive them rather than offend their unspiritual parents or the preacher through whom they professed salvation. They will be impartial, judging every case upon its own merits. They will be careful not to admit one about whose conversion or walk there is any doubt. It is to be feared that some who have been admitted to assemblies, especially children of believing parents, give little or no evidence of ever having been born of God. This is a most serious matter, and should cause deep searchings of heart as to what the consequences of such laxity will be. Satan's masterstroke has always been to produce a "mixed multitude," which he accomplishes by sowing the tares among the wheat, while men are sleeping (Matt. 13:25). "I am persuaded," wrote

C.F. Hogg, "that much evil has resulted, and will result, from the too hasty reception of the children of believers without adequate evidence that they are the children of God. Natural affection and parental sensitivity should not have any weight in the things of the Spirit." May we take these wise and weighty words to heart, ere it is too late.

On the other hand, godly elders will recognise the danger of expecting too much from candidates and of turning away genuine souls just because they have not all the knowledge we think they should possess. It is surely unfair to expect converts, saved perhaps only a few weeks or months, to have an intelligent grasp of truths which it has taken us years to learn. Experience has shown, too, that in some cases those who were unable to state things in a form which commended itself to us, were the ones who afterwards proved to have most heart for Christ.

SATAN'S WHISPERS

We should ever be on our guard against the incessant whispers of Satan to "widen out." Let us adamantly withstand the temptation of higher social prestige, of commercial advantage, or of enhanced popularity. Let not the desire for 'Christian unity,' nor for a wider field of service, turn us from simple, wholehearted obedience to the Word. "Buy the truth and sell it not" (Prov. 23:23), wrote the wisest of men.

BACK TO THE BOOK

We should be students of the Scriptures and

be able to appeal to them to support our views. We must not regard any book of man - the present booklet included - as an infallible manual. The Word of God must be our sole criterion, and it is time for us to get back to the Book, for its authority does not seem to have the place in ministry which it once held. For instance, in a recent magazine article which advocates a very wide line of things, the contributor gives quotations from writings of over 100 years ago, and makes sweeping assertions for which he offers no proof; but never in over 1,500 words does he substantiate any statement or argument by the Word of God: there is not a citation of Scripture in his article from first to last.

It is partly the result of such teaching that there are many assemblies where, under the plea that the Lord's Supper is for all the Lord's people, almost anyone who takes the Christian name is at liberty to partake of it. Such laxity is fraught with peril for the future of assembly life. It should be continually impressed upon believers that we slavishly follow no man, though ever willing to "acknowledge every good thing" that is in any (Philem. 6). By giving the Bible its proper place we are "setting the Lord always before us" (Ps. 16:8), and His warnings in such passages as Acts 20:28-30; 2 Cor. 11:13-15; Gal. 2:4; and Jude 4, surely require to be emphasised in these "last days."

It is true that many of the brethren of over 100 years ago held the Open Table principle. It must not be forgotten, however, that not a few of them lived to change their view, or at least to see that greater care must be exercised in the matter of reception. In his closing years, Mr. J.N. Darby, one of the "early brethren," came to recognise this. "Looseness," he wrote, "is so prevalent now among the denominations, that more care is needed" and again, "If therefore they (candidates for reception) came claiming as a condition liberty to go elsewhere, I could not allow it ... they cannot come in and out just as they please, because the conscience of the assembly is engaged in the matter, and its duty to God, and to Him at whose table they are... There ought to be the strongest, strictest dealing with souls, whether in deed and in truth they believe and confess the divine glory of the Lord Jesus Christ." Now, if Mr Darby felt so burdened about the need for increased care in this matter in his closing years (he died in 1882), when those who claimed to be born again were in almost every case really so, how would he express himself were he alive to-day to witness the rising tide of false profession, apostasy, and lax morality which is sweeping over Christendom?

THE REWARD

Finally, while maintaining diligence in our service for Christ we should be more concerned about pleasing the Lord than about having manifested blessing in that service. What He prizes most is obedience (1 Sam. 15:22), and while it is our responsibility to be faithful, it is God's to give the increase. Success in His work is not assessed merely by present results. For our encouragement let us remember that, provided we keep right in soul, strict obedience to **God's Word** cannot be a barrier to blessing in **God's work,** and will in "that day" win His commendation: "Well done, thou good and faithful servant: thou hast been faithful over a few things, I will make thee ruler over many things: enter thou into the joy of thy lord" (Matt. 25:21).